United States Government Accountability Office

GAO

Report to the Chairman, Subcommittee on Oversight, Committee on Environment and Public Works, U.S. Senate

June 2012

AIR POLLUTION

EPA Needs Better Information on New Source Review Permits

I0415778

GAO

Accountability ★ Integrity ★ Reliability

GAO-12-590

AIR POLLUTION

EPA Needs Better Information on New Source Review Permits

Highlights of GAO-12-590, a report to the Chairman, Subcommittee on Oversight, Committee on Environment and Public Works, U.S. Senate

Why GAO Did This Study

Electricity generating units that burn fossil fuels supply most of the nation's electricity and are major sources of air pollution. Under the Clean Air Act, such units are subject to NSR, a permitting process that applies to (1) units built after August 7, 1977, and (2) existing units that undertake a major modification. Owners of such units must obtain from the appropriate permitting agency a preconstruction permit that sets emission limits and requires the use of certain pollution control technologies. EPA oversees states' implementation of NSR, including reviewing and commenting on draft permits issued by state and local permitting agencies. GAO was asked to examine (1) what information EPA maintains on NSR permits issued to fossil fuel electricity generating units; (2) challenges, if any, that EPA, state, and local agencies face in ensuring compliance with requirements to obtain NSR permits; and (3) what available data show about compliance with requirements to obtain NSR permits. GAO reviewed relevant documentation and interviewed EPA, state, and local officials, as well as representatives from industry, research, and environmental groups.

What GAO Recommends

GAO recommends that EPA, among other actions, consider ways to develop a centralized source of data on NSR permits issued to electricity generating units. EPA expressed its commitment to filling gaps in its data systems, but disagreed with the actions GAO recommended. GAO believes that its recommendations would enhance oversight of NSR permitting and enforcement.

View GAO-12-590 or key components. For more information, contact David C. Trimble at (202) 512-3841 or TrimbleD@gao.gov, or Frank Rusco at (202) 512-3841 or RuscoF@gao.gov.

What GAO Found

The Environmental Protection Agency (EPA) does not maintain complete information on New Source Review (NSR) permits issued to fossil fuel electricity generating units. State and local permitting agencies track the NSR permits they issue, but EPA does not maintain complete or centralized information on permits, despite a 2006 recommendation by the National Research Council that it do so. EPA maintains several databases that compile data on draft and issued NSR permits, but these sources are incomplete and thus cannot be used to identify all of the NSR permits that have been issued nationwide. In addition, EPA has the opportunity to review and comment on every draft NSR permit issued by state and local permitting agencies, but it does not compile data on whether the permitting agencies address EPA's comments in final permits. The absence of more complete information on NSR permitting makes it difficult to know which units have obtained NSR permits or to assess how state and local permitting agencies vary from EPA in their interpretations of NSR requirements.

Officials from EPA, state, and local agencies face challenges in ensuring that owners of fossil fuel electricity generating units comply with requirements to obtain NSR permits. Many of these challenges stem from two overarching issues. First, in some cases it is difficult to determine whether an NSR permit is required. NSR applicability depends on, among other factors, whether a change to a unit qualifies as routine maintenance, repair, and replacement; and whether the change results in a significant net increase in emissions. The rules governing NSR are complex, however, and applicability is determined on a case-by-case basis. Second, it is often difficult to identify noncompliance—instances where unit owners made a major modification without first obtaining an NSR permit—partly because owners of generating units determine whether a permit is needed, and in many cases their determinations are not reviewed by permitting agencies or EPA. State permitting agencies generally issue NSR permits, but EPA typically leads enforcement efforts, since identifying instances of noncompliance involves extensive investigations that go beyond the routine inspections conducted by state and local permitting agencies. EPA identifies NSR noncompliance through a lengthy, resource-intensive process that involves reviewing large amounts of information on units' past emissions and construction activities.

Available data on compliance, although incomplete, suggest that a substantial number of generating units did not comply with requirements to obtain NSR permits. Complete NSR compliance data do not exist for two main reasons: (1) EPA has not yet investigated all generating units for compliance, and (2) NSR compliance is determined at a point in time, and in some cases federal courts have disagreed with EPA about the need for an NSR permit. Nonetheless, EPA has investigated most coal-fired generating units at least once, and has alleged noncompliance at more than half of the units it investigated. Specifically, of the 831 units EPA investigated, 467 units were ultimately issued notices of violation, had complaints filed in court, or were included in settlement agreements. In total, EPA reached 22 settlements covering 263 units, which will require affected unit owners to, among other things, install around $12.8 billion in emissions controls. These settlements will reduce emissions of sulfur dioxide by an estimated 1.8 million tons annually, and nitrogen oxides by an estimated 596,000 tons annually.

_____ United States Government Accountability Office

Contents

Abbreviations

DOJ	Department of Justice
EIA	Energy Information Administration
EPA	Environmental Protection Agency
NSR	New Source Review
OECA	Office of Enforcement and Compliance Assurance
SCR	selective catalytic reduction

United States Government Accountability Office
Washington, DC 20548

June 22, 2012

The Honorable Sheldon Whitehouse
Chairman
Subcommittee on Oversight
Committee on Environment and Public Works
United States Senate

Dear Mr. Chairman:

The efficient and reliable operation of the electricity industry is critical to the health of the U.S. economy. Residential consumers rely on electricity to power their households, and electricity is a key input for businesses that produce trillions of dollars in products and services. The United States depends on a variety of fuels to generate electricity, including fossil fuels (coal, natural gas, and oil), renewable sources (such as wind, solar, and biomass), and nuclear power. Of these, fossil fuels have historically been the primary source of U.S. electricity because of their abundance, reliability, and relatively low cost. Yet in addition to providing about 70 percent of U.S. electricity, electricity generating units at fossil fuel power plants produce substantial amounts of harmful air emissions.[1] In particular, fossil fuel-fired electricity generating units are among the largest emitters of sulfur dioxide and nitrogen oxides, which have been linked to respiratory illnesses and acid rain, as well as of carbon dioxide, the primary greenhouse gas contributing to climate change.

Under the Clean Air Act, the Environmental Protection Agency (EPA) establishes national ambient air quality standards for six pollutants which states, primarily, are responsible for attaining.[2] States attain these standards, in part, by regulating emissions of these pollutants from certain stationary sources, such as electricity generating units. Numerous Clean Air Act requirements apply to electricity generating units, including New

---

[1]Fossil fuel units are responsible for nearly all emissions of carbon dioxide, sulfur dioxide, and nitrogen oxides from the electricity generating sector.

[2]EPA has set national ambient air quality standards for six pollutants, termed "criteria" pollutants: carbon monoxide, lead, nitrogen oxides, ozone, particulate matter, and sulfur oxides.

Source Review (NSR), a permitting process established in 1977.[3] Under NSR, owners of generating units must obtain a preconstruction permit that establishes emission limits and requires the use of certain emissions control technologies.[4] NSR applies to (1) generating units built after August 7, 1977, and (2) existing generating units—regardless of the date built—that seek to undertake a "major modification," a physical or operational change that would result in a significant net increase in emissions of a regulated pollutant.[5] Units built before August 7, 1977, are not required to undergo NSR unless they undertake a major modification. However, EPA's regulatory definition of major modification excludes certain activities; generating units can undertake these activities without obtaining NSR permits or installing any additional controls. For example, activities that qualify as "routine maintenance, repair, and replacement" are not considered major modifications and therefore do not trigger NSR.

Congress allowed units that existed as of August 7, 1977 to defer installation of emissions controls until they made a major modification in the expectation that, over time, all units would either install such controls or shut down, thereby lowering overall emissions. As we reported in April 2012, however, many older units—those that began operating in or before

---

[3]This report focuses solely on fossil fuel electricity generating units and major New Source Review at those units, although NSR also applies to certain other major stationary sources of air pollution, such as other industrial facilities. NSR also applies to minor modifications at major stationary sources, as well as to new and modified minor sources (known as minor NSR).

[4]In areas that meet EPA's national ambient air quality standards—known as attainment areas—the NSR permitting process includes a review for "prevention of significant deterioration" to ensure that the emissions will not exceed maximum allowable increases for three criteria pollutants: nitrogen oxides, sulfur dioxide, and particulate matter. In areas that do not meet the standards—known as nonattainment areas—the permitting process is known as "nonattainment NSR." Throughout this report, the term NSR includes both types of review.

[5]What constitutes a significant net increase in emissions depends on whether the generating unit is located in an attainment or nonattainment area and the type of regulated pollutant being emitted. For example, in all areas, a 100-ton-per-year increase is significant for carbon monoxide, while a 40-ton-per-year increase is significant for nitrogen oxides or sulfur dioxide. In attainment areas, increases of noncriteria regulated pollutants can also be significant.

1978—continue to produce electricity.[6] According to our analysis of EPA data, 1,485 older units (43 percent of fossil fuel units) were still in operation in 2010.[7] A substantial number of these older units did not have emissions controls; for example, 1,201 units (74 percent of older units) did not have controls for sulfur dioxide. In addition, 564 units (38 percent of older units) did not have any controls for nitrogen oxides, and 1,277 units (86 percent of older units) had not installed selective catalytic reduction (SCR) equipment, the type of control most effective at reducing nitrogen oxides. The reduction in emissions from the use of emissions controls can be substantial: SCR equipment, for example, can reduce nitrogen oxides emissions by 70 to 95 percent. Emissions controls can also be expensive; for example, installing SCR equipment in a typical coal-fired generating unit could cost from $108 million to $129 million.

Throughout its history, NSR has been characterized by complexity and controversy, involving disputes between EPA and industry about, among other issues, whether certain changes to generating units qualified for exclusion as routine maintenance, repair, and replacement. In December 2002, EPA finalized revisions to NSR regulations, including exemptions for certain pollution control projects from NSR. These revisions were intended to maximize operating flexibility, improve environmental quality, and promote administrative efficiency, among other aims. In addition, in October 2003, EPA finalized a rule that categorically excluded certain activities from NSR by defining them as "routine maintenance, repair, and replacement." This rule was intended to provide more certainty to generating units and permitting authorities. These NSR reforms, as the two rulemakings were known, provoked considerable controversy. Some states and industry groups agreed with EPA's position, while a number of public health and environmental groups, as well as a group of states primarily from the Mid-Atlantic and Northeast, filed lawsuits challenging the legality of the two rules. Since their issuance, two of the five

---

[6]GAO, *Air Emissions and Electricity Generation at U.S. Power Plants*, GAO-12-545R (Washington, D.C.: Apr. 18, 2012). Analysis is limited to generating units that (1) listed a fossil fuel as a primary fuel; (2) generated electricity in 2010; and (3) had a net summer capacity greater than 25 megawatts, making them subject to EPA's emissions monitoring and reporting requirements.

[7]These 1,485 older units produced 45 percent of the electricity from fossil fuel units in 2010. The remainder was produced by 1,958 newer units (those that began operating after 1978).

provisions in the 2002 rule, as well as the 2003 rule, were struck down in court.[8]

As with many environmental laws, responsibility for implementing NSR, including issuing NSR permits, generally rests with state and local agencies, with oversight by EPA's 10 regional offices and EPA headquarters. Owners or operators of generating units wishing to make major modifications must prepare and submit a permit application to the appropriate state or local permitting agency before construction. The state or local permitting agency determines if the application is complete; develops a draft permit, if one is necessary; notifies EPA and the public of the application; and solicits comments on the draft permit. The permitting agency then issues a final permit, if merited, with responses to comments it received. The permitting agency is to provide EPA with a copy of every permit application, draft permit, and final permit.

EPA administers its NSR oversight and enforcement responsibilities through its headquarters Office of Enforcement and Compliance Assurance, as well as its 10 regional offices. This office monitors compliance, identifies national enforcement concerns and priorities, and provides overall direction on enforcement policies; the office also occasionally takes enforcement action in conjunction with the Department of Justice (DOJ), the agency responsible for handling enforcement cases in federal court. In turn, EPA's regional offices carry out much of EPA's NSR enforcement responsibilities, oversee states' enforcement programs, and implement NSR in certain areas, such as Indian country.[9] Since 1999, EPA has made enforcing NSR among coal-fired electricity generating units a national enforcement priority and has reached several settlements with owners of such units, which have resulted in the installation of emissions controls, unit retirements, agreements to fund environmentally beneficial projects, and tens of millions of dollars in civil penalties.

---

[8]Other revisions to NSR regulations were proposed in 2006 and 2007 but were never finalized, or, if finalized, EPA has stayed their effective date, is considering whether changes to the regulation are necessary, or both. Similarly, a revision finalized in December 2008 has been stayed.

[9]"Indian country" includes all land within the limits of an Indian reservation under the jurisdiction of the United States government, all dependent Indian communities within the borders of the United States, and all Indian allotments, the Indian titles to which have not been extinguished.

This report responds in part to your request for information on the implementation and enforcement of NSR for fossil fuel electricity generating units. Specifically, our objectives were to examine (1) what information EPA maintains on NSR permits issued to fossil fuel electricity generating units; (2) challenges, if any, that EPA, state, and local agencies face in ensuring compliance with requirements to obtain NSR permits; and (3) what available data show about compliance with requirements to obtain NSR permits.

To respond to our objectives, we gathered information from EPA and from selected state and local officials involved in implementing NSR. We selected a nonprobability sample of nine states on the basis of (1) the number of older electricity generating units in the state; (2) the quantity of electricity generated by such units in those states; (3) the volume of sulfur dioxide, nitrogen oxides, and carbon dioxide emitted by units in those states; and (4) the region in which the generating unit was located. The nine states we selected were: Alabama, Georgia, Indiana, Kentucky, Missouri, New York, North Carolina, Ohio, and Pennsylvania. We gathered information from EPA and these selected states on the status of their NSR permitting programs and efforts to collect and maintain relevant data. In addition, we spoke with officials from these states, as well as officials at the four EPA regional offices that oversee these states and EPA's Office of Air and Radiation. In three of the states, some localities are responsible for NSR permitting; we spoke with officials at two of those localities. To assess compliance with NSR, we reviewed relevant documents from EPA, other government agencies, academic and research institutions, environmental organizations, and industry groups. We also interviewed knowledgeable enforcement and compliance officials from EPA headquarters and the four regional offices, as well as officials in selected states and localities, to collect information on EPA's efforts to enforce NSR and track compliance among generating units. In addition, we spoke with stakeholders from academic and research institutions, environmental organizations, and industry groups on these topics. Appendix I provides additional information about our scope and methodology.

We conducted this performance audit from April 2011 to June 2012, in accordance with generally accepted government auditing standards. Those standards require that we plan and perform the audit to obtain sufficient, appropriate evidence to provide a reasonable basis for our findings and conclusions based on our audit objectives. We believe that the evidence obtained provides a reasonable basis for our findings and conclusions based on our audit objectives.

Background

Subject to EPA's oversight, state and local permitting agencies generally administer NSR and operate under one of two arrangements. Under the first arrangement, state and local agencies receive "delegated authority" from EPA under which they implement EPA's NSR regulations. Under the second arrangement, states and localities are also responsible for administering NSR, but instead of implementing EPA's NSR regulations, state and local agencies develop plans, known as state implementation plans, that regulate the construction and modification of stationary sources. These plans provide assurances that the states and localities will have adequate personnel, funding, and authority under state law to carry out the plan, among other provisions. State implementation plans also must include NSR regulations that are at least as stringent as EPA's NSR regulations, although states and local agencies are authorized to include more stringent or additional requirements.[10] States and localities must submit these plans, as well as any revisions to them, to EPA for approval. Once EPA approves the plans, they become federally enforceable requirements.

Although this report focuses on NSR, the Clean Air Act and its implementing regulations subject electricity generating units to additional emissions control requirements. For example, the Acid Rain Program, created by the Clean Air Act Amendments of 1990, established a cap on the amount of sulfur dioxide that may be emitted by electricity generating units nationwide and authorizes those generating units to trade emissions allowances for sulfur dioxide. These facilities must also continuously monitor their emissions and report them to EPA. Furthermore, EPA has recently finalized or proposed several other regulations that will affect many fossil fuel generating units. These regulations include the (1) Mandatory Reporting of Greenhouse Gas rule finalized in 2009, which established reporting requirements for greenhouse gas emissions above certain thresholds; (2) Cross-State Air Pollution Rule, finalized in 2011, which limits sulfur dioxide and nitrogen oxides emissions from a number of states that contribute significantly to nonattainment or interference with maintenance of certain national ambient air quality standards in downwind states; (3) National Emissions Standards for Hazardous Air Pollutants from Coal- and Oil-Fired Electric Utility Steam Generating Units, also known as the Mercury and Air Toxics Standards, which

---

[10]Some states, however, have laws preventing agencies from issuing more stringent regulations.

establish emissions limitations on mercury and other pollutants and was finalized on February 15, 2012; and (4) Standards of Performance for Greenhouse Gas Emissions for New Stationary Sources for Electric Utility Generating Units, proposed in April 2012, which establishes new source performance standards for emissions of carbon dioxide for certain new fossil fuel electricity generating units.[11]

EPA Does Not Maintain Complete Information on Issued NSR Permits or Track the Impact of Its Comments

EPA does not maintain complete information on NSR permits issued to fossil fuel electricity generating units. State and local permitting agencies track the NSR permits they issue, but EPA does not maintain data on these permits in a complete and centralized source of information, which limits the agency's ability to assess the impact of NSR. In addition, EPA has the opportunity to review and comment on every draft NSR permit issued by state and local permitting agencies, but the agency does not compile data on which permitting authorities address EPA's comments. The absence of this information makes it difficult for EPA to measure the impact of its comments and may impede its ability to assess how state and local permitting agencies may differ from EPA in their interpretation of NSR requirements.

EPA Does Not Maintain Complete Data on NSR Permits

EPA does not maintain complete information on NSR permits issued for construction of new fossil fuel electricity generating units or for major modifications to existing units. State and local permitting agencies, which issue NSR permits in most parts of the country, track the NSR permits they issue. (Figure 1 describes the roles of state and local permitting agencies and EPA in issuing NSR permits.) State and local agencies vary widely in the types of data they collect on NSR permits and the systems they use to compile the data. Some states maintain detailed information on NSR permits in electronic form available on publicly accessible websites. For instance, in seven of the nine states where we conducted interviews, state officials maintain information online that can be used to identify the electricity generating units that have received NSR permits, as

---

[11]The Cross-State Air Pollution Rule and the National Emissions Standards for Hazardous Air Pollutants from Coal- and Oil-Fired Electric Utility Steam Generating Units are currently being challenged in court. A federal appeals court has stayed the effective date of the Cross-State Air Pollution Rule while it hears the case. GAO is currently undertaking a study on the effects of these two rules on reliability. The study is expected to be issued in 2012.

well as the requirements of the permits.[12] These data, however, are maintained in different formats across these states and cannot be readily compiled into a complete source of information on NSR permitting for the electricity generating sector.

Figure 1: New Source Review Permitting Process

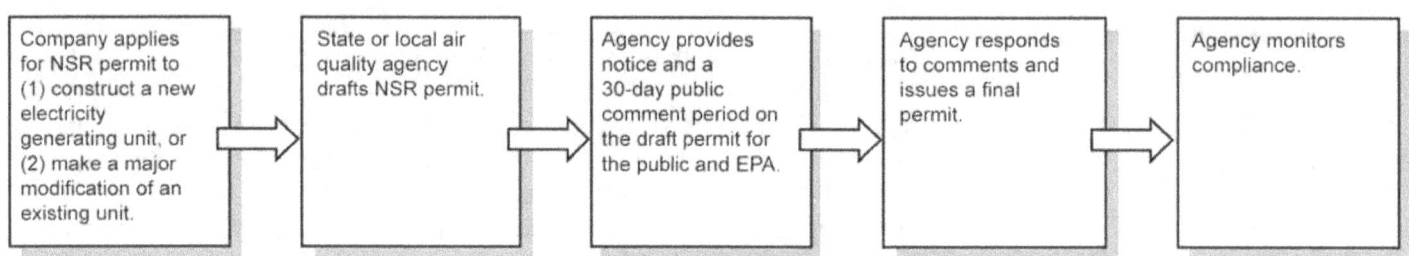

Company applies for NSR permit to (1) construct a new electricity generating unit, or (2) make a major modification of an existing unit. → State or local air quality agency drafts NSR permit. → Agency provides notice and a 30-day public comment period on the draft permit for the public and EPA. → Agency responds to comments and issues a final permit. → Agency monitors compliance.

Source: GAO analysis of EPA data.

In addition to the data collected by state and local permitting agencies, EPA maintains several sources of data on NSR permitting for electricity generating units, but none of these sources are complete. Of the four EPA regional offices we assessed, three offices consolidated NSR permitting data for the states and localities under their oversight.[13] For example, one EPA regional office maintains a spreadsheet to track NSR permits issued over time. The spreadsheet contains information on (1) the type of source applying for the permit, (2) the project under consideration, (3) when a final permit is issued, and (4) what emissions control technologies are required. However, the information maintained by the EPA regional offices is in different formats and is not compiled into a complete, centralized repository of information on NSR permits issued nationwide.

In 2006, the National Research Council recommended that EPA, in conjunction with states and localities, systematically collect data on the full range of NSR permits issued nationwide to stationary sources of air

---

[12]Our review was limited to the NSR permits issued to electricity generating units; state and local permitting agencies may also maintain information on NSR permits issued to other stationary sources.

[13]Regional offices also maintain information on the NSR permits issued by their office, such as to generating units in Indian Country, although officials said that regional offices rarely issue such permits.

pollution, including electricity generating units.[14] In its report the council noted that such information could be useful to stakeholders and decision makers for assessing the broader impacts of NSR regulations, or potential changes to the regulations, on emissions, public health, and energy efficiency. Asked how EPA had responded to this recommendation, officials in EPA's Office of Air and Radiation said it had largely been satisfied by an agency database that tracks the emissions control technologies that have been required by issued NSR permits.[15] However, the database is incomplete; EPA officials said it contains information on approximately 50 percent of issued NSR permits and therefore cannot be used, as recommended by the council, to identify all NSR permits that have been issued nationwide. EPA officials suggested that the database was not complete because some state and local permitting agencies do not enter their information in a timely manner, and others do not report the information at all. In addition, EPA officials noted that the Clean Air Act requires only that states enter permit information for sources in nonattainment areas.[16]

EPA also has a centrally maintained database on NSR permits issued nationwide for sources of greenhouse gases. EPA officials told us this

---

[14]National Research Council, *New Source Review for Stationary Sources of Air Pollution* (Washington, D.C.:2006). In its report, the Council found that no centralized source existed for information on NSR permits issued nationwide. It estimated—using data provided to EPA by state and local permitting authorities that were preliminary, unpublished, and not subjected to review—that from 1997 to 1999 there had been several NSR permits issued for major modifications to existing sources in the combined electricity, gas, and sanitary services sector: 38 for carbon monoxide, 30 for particulate matter, 46 for nitrogen oxides, and zero for sulfur dioxide.

[15]The RACT/BACT/LAER Clearinghouse is a database maintained by EPA's Office of Air and Radiation, which contains information provided by state and local permitting agencies on air pollution control technologies, including technologies required in source-specific permits. The database contains information on over 5,000 air pollution control permit determinations submitted by permitting agencies for several U.S. territories and all 50 states.

[16]*See* 42 U.S.C. § 7503(d). According to EPA officials, in many cases, EPA regional offices also have planning agreements with states stipulating that the state must enter data from all NSR permits into the database. Some regional offices specify a certain time frame by which states must enter the data. These officials said that, as a general matter, the planning agreements are tied to grant funding received by states, and EPA could conceivably withhold funding if a state fails to meet a condition of the agreement. However, with declining budgets and resources at state government levels, officials said that entering data is not always a priority for states, or they may choose to defer entering data until they believe they have a permit that is noteworthy.

database would capture most NSR permitting activity for electricity generating units because such units are major sources of greenhouse gases, in addition to other pollutants. But this database too is incomplete: it has been used only since 2011 and does not contain information on whether the NSR permits include requirements for pollutants other than greenhouse gases. EPA officials mentioned other means of tracking data on NSR permits, but none of these sources can definitively identify the units that have received NSR permits nationwide (see app. II for more information on sources of data on NSR permits).[17]

Because EPA does not maintain comprehensive information on the NSR permits issued to fossil fuel electricity generating units across the nation, the agency does not have complete data on which units have obtained permits, limiting its ability to assess the scope and impact of NSR. Without such data, EPA cannot fully assess what controls have been required or estimate what emissions from generating units may have been averted as a result of NSR requirements.

In addition, the absence of information on NSR permits hinders EPA's ability to efficiently target noncompliance. To identify potential targets for NSR enforcement actions—units that may have made a physical or operational change that resulted in a significant net emissions increase without obtaining a permit—EPA officials we interviewed said they have relied in part on continuous emissions monitoring data required under Title IV of the Clean Air Act. For example, an unusual emissions decrease followed by a sharp increase could signal a temporary plant shutdown to install new equipment. In instances where noncompliance has been suspected, EPA officials we spoke with said they have sometimes consulted relevant state and local permitting authorities to ascertain whether a suspected unit previously received an NSR permit. In other cases, EPA officials told us they have obtained copies of NSR permits by requiring unit owners to provide them through information requests, along with documentation on previously completed work at a suspected unit— making a centralized source of information on NSR permits unnecessary. Nevertheless, without a centralized source of information on NSR permits, EPA enforcement officials cannot readily identify whether a generating unit has obtained an NSR permit, and under what terms,

---

[17] For example, EPA maintains a database aimed at tracking its reviews of draft state-issued permits; the database does not, however, contain information on final permits or their terms.

unless they rely on unit owners or the efforts of state and local permitting agencies to provide this information.

EPA Does Not Track Incorporation of Its Comments into Draft Permits

EPA does not track whether state and local permitting agencies incorporate the agency's comments into final NSR permits for fossil fuel electricity generating units. State and local permitting agencies have the authority to make final permitting decisions, but as part of its oversight responsibilities, EPA has the opportunity to review and comment on every draft NSR permit submitted by state and local permitting agencies.[18] EPA officials said that, when the agency elects to make comments, their reviews often focus on whether and how the permitting authorities conduct the required analyses—for example, whether an appropriate analysis was used to support a proposed emissions control as the best available control technology. The agency's comments are first prepared by regional offices and then reviewed by headquarters to ensure consistency with comments previously issued by the agency. According to EPA officials, EPA's headquarters office maintains a database to track the agency's work and ensure that it delivers comments during the 30-day public comment period. This database includes basic information on the draft permits, but EPA does not use it to track the proposed terms of the permits, the substance of the agency's own comments, whether the draft permits are finalized, or the extent to which state and local agencies incorporated EPA's comments into final permits.

Officials we interviewed in several EPA regional offices said they note the responses of state and local permitting agencies to EPA's comments, but all said that they do not regularly report this information to EPA headquarters. EPA officials also told us that regional officials notify headquarters officials, including members of a working group on the utility industry, when significant areas of concern arise on a final NSR permit for a generating unit. They noted that this information is neither reported systematically nor compiled in a centralized manner, adding that quantifying the impact of all of its comments would be subjective and time-consuming. However, without compiling any information on whether state and local permitting agencies have incorporated its comments into final NSR permits, EPA is limited in its ability to assess the impact of

---

[18]EPA regulations require state and local permitting agencies to give the public at least 30 days to comment on draft NSR permits.

these comments on state and local permitting decisions across the nation. For example, EPA cannot assess the extent to which NSR emissions control requirements imposed by state and local permitting agencies may differ from those suggested by EPA in its comments.[19]

Regulators Face Challenges in Ensuring Compliance with NSR Permitting Requirements

In addition to a lack of comprehensive permitting data, EPA and state and local agencies face other challenges in ensuring that owners of fossil fuel electricity generating units comply with requirements to obtain NSR permits. Many of the challenges stem from two overarching issues: (1) determining whether an NSR permit is required and (2) identifying instances where unit owners should have obtained NSR permits but did not. As a result, EPA's enforcement efforts involve long, resource-intensive investigations.

Determining When NSR Applies Can Be Difficult

A major challenge to EPA, states, and local agencies in ensuring NSR compliance is that it can be difficult for unit owners and regulators to know whether an NSR permit is needed, because NSR's rules governing applicability are complex and because NSR applicability is determined on a case-by-case basis. EPA and state officials we spoke with said that NSR as it applies to new units is fairly straightforward, because newly constructed units generally must obtain NSR permits before starting operation. In contrast, determining what constitutes a major modification of an existing unit, and, thus, what requires an NSR permit, is more complex. Under NSR regulations, owners are to apply for an NSR permit before making any physical or operational change that would result in a significant net increase of emissions. These changes, such as adding new equipment, must be evaluated in the specific context of the unit and its intended use. State officials and industry representatives we interviewed said it can be difficult to determine whether these activities trigger NSR because the two steps for determining applicability—first, whether the unit is making a physical or operational change and, second, whether this change would result in a significant net increase of emissions—are not categorically defined and have changed over time.

---

[19]In states that have adopted their own NSR regulations, these NSR rules may differ from EPA's, although they must be no less stringent than EPA's regulations.

The first step for determining NSR applicability can be complicated because the definition of "physical or operational change" excludes activities that are considered routine maintenance, repair, and replacement. NSR regulations, first finalized in 1978, contained no description or definition of the "routine maintenance" exclusion, instead relying on a case-by-case approach that involves weighing several factors, including the nature, extent, purpose, frequency, and cost of proposed activities. Federal courts, however, have issued inconsistent decisions on whether the factors should be analyzed with respect to industry practice or a particular unit's history. In 2003, in part because of concerns about the case-by-case approach, EPA finalized a rule that categorically excluded certain activities from NSR by defining them as "routine maintenance, repair, and replacement" to provide more certainty to generating units and permitting agencies. Specifically, the rule categorically deemed certain replacement activities to be routine maintenance, repair, and replacement if certain conditions were met, such as replacement activities' costs not exceeding a specified threshold. In 2006, however, a federal appeals court struck down this rule because it was contrary to the plain language of the Clean Air Act.

As a result, a case-by-case approach is still used to determine which activities qualify for the exclusion. Several state officials and industry representatives we interviewed said that the case-by-case approach makes it difficult to know when NSR applies. A number of industry representatives also said that uncertainty around NSR applicability can deter owners from making improvements to units that would improve efficiency. One senior EPA enforcement official we interviewed, however, noted that NSR regulations are written broadly to cover many disparate industries and said it would not be possible for EPA to develop detailed regulations tailored to each industry. One state official we spoke with also said that attempts to more precisely specify what activities are considered routine maintenance might not be worthwhile, since EPA's previous efforts to do so were struck down in court.

The second step in determining NSR applicability—assessing whether a change results in a significant net increase in emissions—presents additional complications. Like the routine maintenance exclusion, regulations governing what constitutes an increase in emissions have been subject to litigation, leading to changes in the process used to measure emissions increases over time. For example, in 1992, in response to a court decision, EPA finalized a regulation changing how future emissions from generating units are to be calculated. Rather than calculating future emissions based on a unit's potential to emit, under the revised regulation, future emissions are calculated based, in part, on the maximum emissions that can be generated while operating the unit as it is intended to be operated and as it is normally operated. Some state officials and industry representatives we interviewed said that calculating emissions increases can be challenging because the regulations are complex, and EPA's interpretation has changed over time. NSR's complexity can be particularly difficult for owners of smaller generating units who may lack the legal and technical expertise to properly comply with NSR, according to an EPA official and industry representative we interviewed. EPA officials acknowledged that the process is not always simple, but they also noted that it is much easier for companies to make these calculations than for permitting agencies to verify them, since permitting agencies are less familiar with—and have less access to—information about a generating unit, its activities, and its data systems, than the companies.

According to several state officials and industry representatives we interviewed, assessing whether a change results in a significant net increase in emissions can also be complicated because EPA regulations authorize certain emissions increases to be excluded from this assessment—specifically, those emissions increases that are attributable to growth in demand.[20] Several state officials we interviewed said that some owners have had difficulty distinguishing between emissions increases due to projected growth in demand and emissions increases resulting from the change to the unit, a process made more difficult because EPA has not offered clarification or guidance regarding this exclusion. One senior EPA enforcement official disagreed with this assessment, noting that utilities commonly employ models that help project demand as a way to guide their operations and investment decisions. According to this official, EPA's approach is based on methods already widely employed throughout the electricity sector.

EPA and state agency officials, who are responsible for verifying owners' calculations when they apply for a permit or seek guidance on NSR applicability, said that verifications are further complicated by other NSR provisions that exclude certain activities from NSR. For example, a

---

[20]The portion of the generating unit's emissions post-project that could have been accommodated by the generating unit at a certain time before the proposed change, and that are also unrelated to the project, including any increased utilization due to demand growth, can be excluded from the calculation of emissions increases.

GAO-12-590 EPA's Implementation of New Source Review

change that significantly increases a generating unit's emissions will not trigger NSR if it does not cause a net increase in emissions. Specifically, an NSR permit is not required if the increase in emissions resulting from a change is offset by certain contemporaneous emissions reductions, a process called "netting." EPA has defined "contemporaneous" as within 5 years before construction on the change commences, although states can define the term differently. Thus, an owner could compensate for an emissions increase in a given year by subtracting emissions decreases that were made in the previous 5 years, although any other emissions increases during that 5-year period must also have been included in the calculation. Several state agency officials we spoke with said that unit owners often pursue this option so they do not have to obtain an NSR permit and install costly emissions controls. Several EPA and state officials we interviewed also said, however, that it can be difficult to verify that calculations are valid, in part because they must rely on information provided by the unit owners. Some of these officials said it can be difficult to determine what types of emissions reductions and increases may be aggregated together under the netting option.[21] One EPA regional office official said that, overall, options such as netting complicate and lengthen the permitting process because they require unit owners to submit additional documentation that the regulator must in turn review.

To aid owners and regulators in determining when NSR should apply, EPA and state officials identified several sources of available guidance, including the following:

- *Consultations with state and local agencies.* Before seeking a permit, owners of units can request assistance from state and local permitting agencies in determining whether NSR applies. Some state agency officials said that unit owners in their state regularly seek guidance, particularly on how to qualify for one of NSR's exclusions. However, other EPA and state officials we spoke with said that such requests are uncommon; many unit owners may hesitate to contact a regulatory agency because regulators may have a different interpretation of NSR that could require them to install costly emissions controls.

---

[21]In September 2006, EPA proposed a rule clarifying how emissions decreases from a project may be included in the calculation to determine if a significant emissions increase will result. EPA did not finalize the rule.

- *EPA's 1990 draft NSR workshop manual.* Several state agency officials we spoke with said they rely on a draft EPA manual from 1990 issued as guidance for implementing the federal NSR permitting process, although the manual was never finalized and has not been updated.

- *Regionally maintained databases.* Through one of its regional offices, EPA maintains an online database containing more than 600 EPA-issued policy and guidance documents. Several EPA and state officials we interviewed said that the database was helpful in providing current information on how to apply NSR, although one state official said that these determinations are not always consistent.

- *Court decisions.* Several EPA and state permitting officials we interviewed said they rely primarily on court rulings for guidance on interpreting NSR regulations to ensure that their determinations are up-to-date.

EPA officials said that the agency's ability to generate comprehensive, nationwide guidance is limited because of the case-by-case nature of NSR, ongoing litigation, and the variation in NSR requirements across states. For example, some states and localities have adopted NSR requirements that are more stringent than the federal regulations. Furthermore, some states' regulations differ because they have not revised their state implementation plans to incorporate the 2002 NSR reforms or had those revisions approved by EPA.

Identifying NSR Noncompliance Requires Long Investigations

The second major challenge EPA and state and local agencies face in ensuring compliance with NSR is that it is often difficult for regulators to identify noncompliance—that is, instances where owners did not obtain NSR permits before making major modifications to their generating units. According to several EPA officials we interviewed, identifying noncompliance can be challenging because unit owners—not regulatory agencies—have responsibility for determining whether they need an NSR permit. Most owners do not ultimately obtain NSR permits before making changes to their units, according to EPA officials we interviewed, because the owners determine that the changes fall under one of NSR's exclusions, such as routine maintenance, or because they offset emissions increases through netting. These unit owners are generally not required to notify EPA or state or local permitting agencies when they use these exclusions. Therefore, EPA would not review the owners' determinations unless (1) the owner proactively sought a permit and the state or local permitting agency determined that an NSR permit was required or (2) EPA initiated an investigation. In instances where a unit did not apply for and receive a permit as required, it can take EPA several years to identify the noncompliance and take corrective action. Moreover, under an EPA rule finalized in 2007, known as the "reasonable possibility recordkeeping" rule, a unit owner who determines that a change will not trigger NSR is not required to keep records of the change and its resulting emissions unless the owner believes there is a reasonable possibility that the change could result in a significant emissions increase, and other conditions are met.[22] According to one state official we interviewed, this rule may complicate efforts to identify noncompliance because EPA and state regulators generally have to retroactively determine whether an NSR permit should have been obtained for past activities, and without the benefit of company records, such a determination is difficult.

According to EPA and state officials we interviewed, state and local permitting agencies are generally not well positioned to identify noncompliance. State and local permitting agencies routinely inspect units, but officials told us these inspections focus on compliance with the terms of existing operating permits, not on whether an owner failed to obtain a permit. Several EPA and state officials told us that, given the complexity of most units, routine compliance inspections are not well suited to detect NSR violations, in part because it is difficult to distinguish work that might be considered a major modification from other work that is routine. According to one EPA official, to identify noncompliance with NSR, agency investigators need to identify what changes have already occurred; gather information on the nature of these changes; and determine whether NSR should have applied at the time the changes occurred, considering all possible exclusions and other factors. EPA officials we spoke with said that this process requires investigators to analyze information on historic emissions and a large volume of records on work conducted over the course of a unit's life. According to these and other EPA officials, such extensive review would not be possible during routine compliance inspections. Several state and EPA officials we spoke with also said that, given the complexity and case-by-case nature of NSR, state and local agencies generally do not have the resources—and in some cases expertise—to detect noncompliance. As result, several state

---

[22]This 2007 final rule was a clarification of a 2002 NSR reform regulation that the D.C. Circuit Court remanded to EPA in 2005. EPA is currently considering whether changes to the regulation are necessary and a litigating a case about the rule.

officials we spoke with said they rely on EPA to identify instances of noncompliance with NSR.

EPA has therefore taken a lead role in enforcing NSR, beginning in the mid-1990s and continuing to the present. In 1996, EPA began targeting older, coal-fired generating units for compliance assessments and, on the basis of its investigations, alleged that several of the largest coal-fired electricity generating units in the country had violated NSR provisions by making major modifications without obtaining an NSR permit. In 1999 and early 2000, after receiving a number of cases from EPA, DOJ filed seven enforcement actions in U.S. federal courts in what is known as EPA's Coal-Fired Power Plant Enforcement Initiative. For their part, owners of units targeted by the NSR enforcement initiative contended that, among other things, their projects should have qualified for the routine maintenance exclusion. Nonetheless, almost all of these cases ultimately resulted in settlements mandating the installation of emissions controls and civil penalties. Since then, EPA and DOJ have continued this enforcement initiative and secured additional settlements for alleged noncompliance with NSR. According to EPA, steps to develop an NSR enforcement case include:

1. *Section 114 requests.* Under Section 114 of the Clean Air Act, EPA may obtain information from owners of generating units to determine whether violations have occurred. Such information includes detailed cost information on capital construction projects suspected to be NSR violations. According to EPA officials, collecting and reviewing such information can take several months to over a year.

2. *Settlement negotiations.* After reviewing generating units' records, EPA determines whether NSR violations have occurred. If EPA determines that the unit is not in compliance, it will notify owners of generating units and encourage the owner to install emissions controls. EPA initially tries to resolve noncompliance through a settlement.

3. *Referral.* If settlement negotiations are unsuccessful, EPA will determine whether enough evidence exists to refer the case to DOJ for potential litigation. DOJ then reviews the accumulated evidence and determines whether there is merit to file suit against the company. Before filing the case in court, DOJ generally discusses the matter with the owner in a further attempt to settle.

According to EPA and DOJ officials, EPA's investigations for NSR compliance, and subsequent enforcement actions, take a long time to conclude and involve substantial EPA resources. In instances where EPA's investigations have uncovered suspected violations, it can take years to litigate a case or bring it to conclusion through a settlement. Specifically, the 22 settlements resulting from EPA's enforcement initiative took, on average, 7 years to conclude. According to several industry representatives we interviewed, these efforts have also placed a large burden on owners and operators of generating units, given the amount of information required on past activities at the unit.

Available Data on NSR Compliance Are Not Complete but Suggest Substantial Noncompliance

Available data, while not complete, suggest that a substantial number of generating units have not complied with requirements to obtain NSR permits. Complete data on NSR compliance do not exist for two primary reasons. First, EPA has not yet investigated all electricity generating units for compliance with requirements to obtain NSR permits. Second, NSR compliance is determined at a point in time, and EPA's interpretation of compliance has, in some cases, differed from that of federal courts. Nonetheless, EPA has investigated a majority of coal-fired generating units, and data from these investigations suggest that a substantial number of generating units have not complied.

Complete Data on Unit Compliance with NSR Are Not Available

From our review of relevant documentation and EPA-provided data, we identified two primary reasons why complete data on NSR compliance are not available. First, EPA has not yet investigated all generating units for NSR compliance, and second, available data do not provide a complete picture of compliance.

EPA has investigated most—but not all—coal-fired generating units for compliance with NSR at least once. According to our review of EPA-provided documents and data, EPA has investigated 831 generating units at least once since it began its Coal-Fired Power Plant Enforcement Initiative. These 831 units represent about 81 percent of all coal-fired units that generated electricity in 2010 and about 24 percent of all fossil fuel-fired units (those using coal, natural gas, or oil) that produced electricity in 2010.[23] Most natural gas units—as well as some smaller coal-fired units—have not been investigated by EPA. According to EPA officials we interviewed, the agency has focused most of its NSR compliance efforts on large, coal-fired units because they produce dramatically higher levels of harmful air emissions.

Data on units investigated by EPA are not conclusive because compliance is determined at a point in time; therefore, subsequent changes to the unit could affect its future compliance with NSR. NSR is required each time an existing generating unit undertakes a major modification. Thus, an owner of electricity generating unit that has obtained an NSR permit in the past—or was subject to an EPA investigation—is not exempt from the requirement to obtain an NSR permit for any future major modifications.[24] Moreover, allegations of noncompliance stemming from EPA's investigations do not necessarily mean that a violation has occurred, because in some cases federal courts have ultimately disagreed with EPA about the need for an NSR permit. Given these issues, it is difficult to provide a comprehensive assessment of NSR compliance at any given time.

EPA Has Found Noncompliance at a Majority of Units It Has Investigated

These limitations notwithstanding, data on generating units investigated by EPA shed some light on overall compliance with NSR among electricity generating units. Among the 831 generating units it has investigated through its Coal-Fired Power Plant Enforcement Initiative, EPA has alleged NSR noncompliance at a substantial number. Specifically, EPA has alleged noncompliance—documented through notices of violation, complaints filed in court, or settlements—at 467 generating units, around 56 percent of the units it has investigated.[25] These 467 units investigated by EPA represent approximately 45 percent

---

[23]Analysis is based on a universe of 3,443 electricity generating units in the U.S. that (1) listed a fossil fuel as a primary fuel, (2) had a net summer capacity greater than 25 megawatts, and (3) produced electricity in 2010.

[24]Although units must undergo NSR review for major modifications, some of the settlement agreements EPA has reached with electricity generating units include a provision precluding EPA, in certain circumstances, from suing the owner for making a major modification and not undergoing NSR.

[25]In the settlements, companies generally denied the alleged violations and maintained their compliance with the Clean Air Act but agreed to settle to avoid the costs and uncertainties of litigation and improve the environment.

of coal-fired units that produced electricity in 2010, and about 14 percent of all fossil fuel-fired units that produced electricity in 2010.[26]

According to EPA, the Coal-Fired Power Plant Enforcement Initiative is perhaps the most comprehensive and coordinated enforcement effort under the Clean Air Act to date. The initiative has led to 22 settlements covering a total of 263 units, or approximately 32 percent of the units EPA has investigated. According to our analysis of EPA data, the settlements will require affected unit owners to install and operate emissions controls costing an estimated $12.8 billion in total and levy civil penalties totaling around $80 million. Some companies are also required to fund environmentally beneficial projects, such as restoring watersheds and forests in national parks. These settlements are projected to reduce sulfur dioxide emissions by more than 1.8 million tons annually and nitrogen oxides emissions by about 596,000 tons annually.[27] In some cases, EPA reached companywide settlements in which companies agreed to put emissions controls on units constituting most of their production capacity. Two of the largest settlements—with American Electric Power and the Tennessee Valley Authority—represent 105 units, around 40 percent of the total, and about $8.6 billion in control costs, or around two-thirds of the total. A senior Department of Justice official we interviewed said that, in addition to the 22 concluded settlements, 7 additional NSR cases are in various stages of litigation. See appendix III for more details on EPA's concluded NSR settlements.

Conclusions

Ensuring compliance with NSR presents significant challenges for EPA, and state and local permitting agencies. Unit owners—not regulators—are responsible for determining when an NSR permit is needed, and, because of NSR's complex requirements, these determinations are not always straightforward. The complexity and case-by-case nature of NSR requirements also mean that NSR violations are difficult to detect, once they occur. State and local agencies generally do not have the resources to identify NSR violations and therefore rely on EPA to enforce NSR. Although available data on NSR compliance are not conclusive, the

---

[26]Analysis is based on a universe of 3,443 electricity generating units that (1) listed a fossil fuel as a primary fuel, (2) had a net summer capacity greater than 25 megawatts, and (3) produced electricity in 2010.

[27]These reductions are to be phased in over an agreed-upon time frame, often 10 years.

substantial number of generating units EPA investigations have allegedly found to be noncompliant suggests that many generating units have not obtained NSR permits as required. Addressing NSR's complexity and improving compliance could reduce the need for long and resource-intensive enforcement actions and more effectively protect air quality by averting emissions before they occur. Yet EPA's ability to simplify NSR or develop comprehensive, nationwide guidance is limited for several reasons, including the case-by-case nature of NSR applicability, ongoing litigation, and the variation in NSR requirements across states.

Nonetheless, EPA has an opportunity to improve its efforts by collecting more comprehensive NSR permitting data. Several EPA regional offices maintain some information on the NSR permits issued by the state and local permitting agencies in their regions, but this information is in different formats and not compiled by EPA into a complete and centralized source of information on NSR permits issued nationwide, as recommended by the National Research Council in 2006. More complete information on NSR permitting would help EPA and external parties gauge the extent to which fossil fuel generating units have obtained NSR permits and help inform enforcement efforts that have already found widespread alleged noncompliance.

In cases where unit owners apply for permits before making physical or operational changes that would result in a significant net increase of emissions, EPA plays an important role because it has an opportunity to comment on every draft NSR permit under consideration by state and local permitting agencies and to influence decisions about the appropriate level of pollution control, among others. A key benefit of EPA's involvement in the permitting process is that the agency can review and comment on permits issued in different geographic areas and assess various aspects of draft permits, including the level of emissions control required. Because emissions controls can cost owners and operators of generating units hundreds of millions of dollars, EPA's review of the required level of emissions control is critically important. Although EPA and headquarters staff devote resources to commenting on draft permits, EPA does not track whether state and local permitting agencies incorporate the agency's comments. Without such information, EPA cannot fully assess the extent to which state and local agencies incorporate its comments in NSR permits or the extent to which emissions control requirements imposed by state and local permitting agencies reflect suggestions made by EPA in its comments.

Recommendations for Executive Action

To help improve EPA's implementation of NSR, we recommend that the EPA Administrator direct the entities responsible for implementing and enforcing NSR—specifically, the Office of Enforcement and Compliance Assurance, Office of Air Quality Planning and Standards, and EPA regions—to take the following two actions:

- Working with EPA regions and state and local permitting agencies, consider ways to develop a centralized source of information on NSR permits issued to fossil fuel electricity generating units, and

- Using appropriate methods, such as sampling or periodic assessments, develop a process for evaluating the effects of its comments on draft NSR permits.

Agency Comments and Our Evaluation

We provided a draft of this report to the Department of Energy, the Department of Justice, and Environmental Protection Agency (EPA). The Department of Energy said they had no comments on the report's findings and recommendations. The Department of Justice provided technical comments, which we incorporated as appropriate. EPA provided written comments, a copy of which can be found in appendix IV. In its written comments, EPA agreed with the importance of having good systems for tracking and compiling information to efficiently and effectively administer its programs, while enhancing accountability and transparency, but disagreed with the need for the actions called for in our recommendations.

Regarding our first recommendation that EPA work with state and local permitting authorities to consider ways to develop a centralized source of information on permits issued to electric generating units, EPA said that it believes it has a number of permit tracking mechanisms in place, and raised four concerns about our recommendation. First, EPA said that it has maintained a centralized permit information database for many years—the RACT/BACT/LAER Clearinghouse, which is capable of capturing and sharing information on NSR permits that have been issued. However, EPA acknowledged that this database is incomplete—including about half of issued NSR permits—primarily because, in some areas, state and local agencies are not required to enter information about the permits they issue. Nonetheless, EPA said it is taking steps to improve participation. We continue to believe that comprehensive permitting data would enable EPA, Congress, and other interested parties to better understand the scope and impact of NSR.

Second, EPA said that its regional offices track NSR permitting by the states in their jurisdiction and that the agency believes it is most appropriate for the regional offices, rather than headquarters, to be responsible for this information. However, our work found that the tracking of NSR permits by EPA's regional office varied in completeness. For example, of the four regions we included in our sample, one region had a robust system for tracking issued NSR permits, and one had no system at all. EPA also said that its regional offices provide oversight of state and local agencies and that an EPA-wide compilation of permit data would be redundant, add costs, and provide little benefit to its oversight function. We continue to believe that a centralized source of complete information on NSR permits would enhance EPA's oversight of state and local permitting agencies and help ensure consistency across regions. EPA headquarters could build on the ongoing efforts of some regional offices and develop more complete data using a simple, low-cost system. For example, we found that two regional offices use a spreadsheet to compile and maintain basic data on permits issued by state and local agencies. Additionally, we believe that any costs incurred in developing more comprehensive data should be considered relative to the benefits that could accrue from having better information on the universe of permitted facilities including, as noted by the National Research Council, the ability to assess the impact of policy changes.

Third, EPA said that a centralized database of all NSR permits would not help most members of the public because most members of the public are interested in permits issued to specific facilities rather than the entire universe of all permits issued. Our report focused on the importance of more complete data to enhance programwide oversight of NSR permitting and targeting of enforcement efforts. More complete data could potentially assist the public and other interested parties in understanding the extent of NSR permitting for individual facilities, but this was not the basis of our findings and recommendations. We continue to believe that a centralized source of permitting data is important for EPA's oversight of state and local permitting agencies and to enhance its enforcement efforts.

Fourth, EPA questioned the value of more comprehensive information in targeting noncompliance with requirements to obtain permits. Specifically, EPA said that identifying noncompliance involves targeting facilities that should have obtained permits but did not and that information on facilities that have obtained permits would not assist in these efforts. Moreover, EPA said that getting data on noncompliant sources is time- and resource-intensive. We continue to believe that compiling complete information on facilities that have obtained permits could help identify facilities that have not obtained permits and enhance targeting of these facilities for potential noncompliance. We also believe that understanding which facilities have obtained permits as required could decrease these time and resource demands because the agency would have a better starting point for identifying noncompliance.

Regarding our second recommendation that EPA develop a process for evaluating the effect of its comments on issued permits, the agency said that its regional offices already do so and described the interactions between these offices and state and local agencies during the permitting process. EPA also said that its regional offices already conduct oversight of state and local permitting agencies, including whether these agencies adequately address EPA's comments on draft permits. We acknowledge these efforts in the report and believe that, as part of its overall oversight of nationwide permitting efforts, EPA headquarters could benefit from a broader and more comprehensive assessment of the extent to which its comments on draft permits were adequately considered and incorporated. Because the terms of issued permits can result in the installation of pollution controls that cost hundreds of millions of dollars, it is important to conduct higher level review of issued permits to identify variability in the terms of issued permits across geographic areas. We therefore continue to believe that implementing this recommendation would enhance oversight of NSR permitting nationwide and that EPA has an opportunity to build on the information already collected through the oversight activities of its regional offices.

EPA also provided technical comments that we incorporated as appropriate.

As agreed with your office, unless you publicly announce the contents of this report earlier, we plan no further distribution until 30 days from the report date. At that time, we will send copies to the appropriate congressional committees, the Administrator of EPA, and other interested parties. In addition, the report will be available at no charge on the GAO website at http://www.gao.gov.

If you or your staff have any questions about this report, please contact David Trimble at (202) 512-3841 or trimbled@gao.gov or Frank Rusco at (202) 512-3841 or ruscof@gao.gov. Contact points for our Offices of Congressional Relations and Public Affairs may be found on the last page of this report. GAO staff who made key contributors to this report are listed in appendix V.

Sincerely yours,

David C. Trimble
Director, Natural Resources and Environment

Frank Rusco
Director, Natural Resources and Environment

Appendix I: Scope and Methodology

To assess what information the Environmental Protection Agency (EPA) maintains on New Source Review (NSR) permits issued for fossil fuel electricity generating units, we gathered information from EPA and selected states on the status of their NSR permitting programs and efforts to collect and maintain permitting data. We selected a nonprobability sample of nine states on the basis of (1) the number of older electricity generating units in the state; (2) the quantity of electricity generated by such units in those states; (3) the volume of sulfur dioxide, nitrogen oxides, and carbon dioxide emitted by units in those states; and (4) the region in which the generating unit was located.[1] We obtained these data from the Ventyx Velocity Suite EV Market-Ops database, a proprietary database containing consolidated energy and emissions data from EPA, the Energy Information Administration (EIA), and other sources. To assess the reliability of the Ventyx data, we reviewed documentation provided by Ventyx and tested key variables to verify their accuracy and determined the Ventyx data to be sufficiently reliable for our purposes. The nine states we selected were Alabama, Georgia, Indiana, Kentucky, Missouri, New York, North Carolina, Ohio, and Pennsylvania. To assess how permitting information is collected and used, we reviewed relevant documentation from these nine states and from EPA. We also interviewed permitting officials from these nine states, the four EPA regional offices that oversee these states, EPA's Office of Air and Radiation, its Office of Inspector General, and its Office of Enforcement and Compliance Assurance. In three of the states, some localities are responsible for NSR permitting; we also spoke with officials at two of those localities, which we selected on the basis of the number of older units in their jurisdictions.

To examine what challenges, if any, EPA, state, and local agencies face in ensuring compliance by electricity generating units with requirements to obtain NSR permits, we reviewed relevant provisions of the Clean Air Act and NSR regulations; guidance and other information on implementing NSR maintained by EPA; and literature on NSR from government agencies, academic and research institutions, environmental organizations, and industry groups. We also interviewed knowledgeable officials and stakeholders from these agencies and institutions, as well as officials from the selected states and localities.

---

[1]Because we used a nonprobability sample, the results we obtained from electricity generating units in these states are not generalizeable to such units in all states; nonetheless, these results did help us understand how NSR is implemented and enforced in different states.

To review what available data show about compliance with requirements to obtain NSR permits, we reviewed information published by EPA on the estimated rate of noncompliance by industrial sectors. We also reviewed information on EPA's enforcement activities maintained by enforcement officials in EPA's Office of Enforcement and Compliance Assurance, including (1) data on notices of violation sent to owners of generating units alleging noncompliance with NSR; (2) lawsuits filed in court for alleged NSR violations; and (3) information on the settlements concluded by EPA and the Department of Justice with owners of generating units, which ended or prevented lawsuits alleging noncompliance. To assess the reliability of the EPA-provided data, we interviewed knowledgeable agency officials and tested key variables to verify their accuracy. We determined these data to be sufficiently reliable for the purposes of our analysis. We also interviewed knowledgeable enforcement and compliance officials from EPA's headquarters Office of Enforcement and Compliance Assurance and four regional offices.

We conducted this performance audit from April 2011 to June 2012, in accordance with generally accepted government auditing standards. Those standards require that we plan and perform the audit to obtain sufficient, appropriate evidence to provide a reasonable basis for our findings and conclusions based on our audit objectives. We believe that the evidence obtained provides a reasonable basis for our findings and conclusions based on our audit objectives.

Appendix II: Comparison of Available Databases of NSR Permits for Electricity Generating Units

Table 1: Comparison of Available NSR Permit Databases

Database	Main purpose	Limitations
EPA control technology clearinghouse	To enable state permitting agencies, EPA regional offices, and regulated sources to assess EPA's determinations on past NSR applications with respect to required emissions control technologies	By EPA's estimates, captures about 50 percent of permits
State databases or permit records	To assist states in keeping records of their own permitting activity	Do not consolidate permits for regionwide or nationwide assessment; state systems to track permits vary widely
Regional databases	To inform regulated sources and the public on the status of permitting activity	Data limited to regional jurisdiction; completeness of data varies by region
Office of Air Quality Planning and Standards greenhouse gas permitting database	To assist EPA's headquarters permitting division in tracking NSR permits related to greenhouse gases following 2010 greenhouse gas rule	Tracks permits issued since 2011, after greenhouse gas rule took effect; may exclude NSR permits for some activities, such as coal handling, that affect particulate matter but not greenhouse gases
Office of Air Quality Planning and Standards comment letter database	To help EPA ensure consistency in its comments on draft permits and to meet comment deadlines	Does not track whether draft permits are finalized, or their terms
Region 7 coal-fired utility database	To track permits issued to coal-fired generating units from 2000 to 2010	Database only covers newly constructed coal-fired units for a limited time period
Region 4 combustion turbine database	To track permits issued to combustion turbine units from the early 1990s onward	Database only covers combustion turbine units, most commonly natural-gas-fired units, and is no longer being updated

Source: GAO analysis.

Appendix III: Concluded NSR Settlements

Table 2: Concluded NSR Settlements Involving Electricity Generating Units

Dollar in millions

Company	Date settlement lodged	Number of units involved	Civil penalties	Estimated control costs	Environmentally beneficial projects	Emissions reductions (tons per year) Sulfur dioxide	Nitrogen oxides
Tampa Electric Company	2/19/2000	10	$3.5	$1,000	$10.5[a]	70,000	53,000
Public Service Enterprise Group	1/24/2002 and 11/30/2006	4	7.4	337	9.25	36,194	18,807
Alcoa, Inc.	3/27/2003	3	1.5	330	2.5	52,900	15,480
Virginia Electric and Power Company	4/17/2003	20	5.3	1,200	13.9	176,500	60,400
Wisconsin Electric Power Company	4/29/2003	23	3.2	600	22.5[b]	72,300	32,600
Southern Indiana Gas and Electric Company	6/6/2003	3	0.6	30	2.5	6,400	4,200
South Carolina Public Service Authority	3/16/2004	12	2	400	4.5	37,500	29,500
Illinois Power Company and Dynegy Midwest Generation	3/7/2005	10	9	500	15	39,500[c]	14,800[d]
Ohio Edison	3/18/2005 and 8/11/2009	29	8.5	1,100	25	171,500	31,050
Alabama Power	4/25/2006	2	0.1	200	4.9	22,790	4,940
Minnkota Power Cooperative	4/26/2006	3	0.85	100	5	23,561	9,458
Nevada Power	6/13/2007	4	0.3	60	0.4	N/A	2,300
Eastern Kentucky Power Cooperative	7/2/2007	6	0.75	600	47	54,000	8,000
American Electric Power	10/9/2007	46	15	4,600	60	654,000	159,000
Salt River Project	8/12/2008	2	0.95	400	4	14,303	6,789
Kentucky Utilities	2/3/2009	1	1.4	135	3	28,500	3,000
Duke Energy	12/22/2009	4	1.75	85	6.25	35,000	N/A
Westar Energy	1/25/2010	3	3	500	6	60,000	18,600
American Municipal Power	5/18/2010	4	0.85	0	15	30,600	3,160
Hoosier Energy	7/23/2010	4	0.95	275[e]	5	19,827	1,845
Northern Indiana Public Service Company	1/13/2011	11	3.5	600	9.5	46,000	18,000
Tennessee Valley Authority	4/14/2011	59	10	4,000[f]	350	225,757	115,977
Total		**263**	**$80**	**$12,777**	**$589**	**1,837,632**	**596,106**

Source: GAO analysis of EPA data.

[a]EPA estimated the costs of environmentally beneficial projects at $10 to $11 million.

[b]EPA estimated the costs of environmentally beneficial projects at $20 to $25 million.

[c]EPA estimated reductions in sulfur dioxide emissions of 39,500 tons per year compared with 2003 emissions and 283,000 tons per year compared with 1999 emissions.

[d]EPA estimated reductions in nitrogen oxides emissions of 14,800 tons per year compared with 2003 emissions and 58,200 tons per year compared with 1999 emissions.

[e]EPA estimated control costs at $250 to $300 million.

[f]EPA estimated control costs at $3 to $5 billion.

Appendix IV: Comments from the Environmental Protection Agency

UNITED STATES ENVIRONMENTAL PROTECTION AGENCY
WASHINGTON, D.C. 20460

JUN 1 5 2012

Mr. David C. Trimble
Director, Natural Resources and Environment
U.S. General Accountability Office
441 G Street, NW
Washington, D.C. 20548

Dear Mr. Trimble:

Thank you for the opportunity to review and comment on GAO's draft report "Air Pollution: EPA Needs Better Information on New Source Review Permits." As stated in the draft report, GAO's objectives in this review of the New Source Review (NSR) program were to examine (1) what information the EPA maintains on NSR permits issued to fossil fuel electricity generating units; (2) challenges, if any, that the EPA, state and local agencies face in ensuring compliance with requirements to obtain NSR permits; and (3) what available data show about compliance with requirements to obtain NSR permits. The draft report encompasses both the nonattainment NSR permitting program and the Prevention of Significant Deterioration (PSD) permitting program.

I am responding on behalf of the EPA offices that participated in this review – the Office of Air and Radiation, the Office of Enforcement Compliance and Assurance and four of the EPA's Regional Offices. Below, I am providing our comments on the report's two recommendations. In the enclosure, I am offering a number of technical comments/corrections pertaining to the report.

We agree that having good systems for compiling and tracking information is important for the efficient and effective administration of our programs and helps provide transparency and accountability. The EPA is committed to improving the systems we have and to filling important gaps as we find them. Our reactions to GAO's specific recommendations below simply reflect different views about how those goals are best accomplished in the specific context of NSR permitting.

Recommendation: *Working with EPA regions and state and local permitting authorities, consider ways to develop a centralized source of information on NSR permits issued to fossil fuel electric generating units.*

Response: Based on the draft report, the objective of this recommendation appears to be twofold: (1) improved oversight of the permitting of facilities by the EPA Regional Offices and by state and local agencies, and (2) better identification of instances and patterns of noncompliance with NSR requirements by sources. In general, the EPA believes that we already have a number of permit tracking mechanisms in place that meet these objectives.

Internet Address (URL) • http://www.epa.gov
Recycled/Recyclable • Printed with Vegetable Oil Based Inks on 100% Postconsumer, Process Chlorine Free Recycled Paper

First of all, the EPA has maintained a centralized permit information database for many years. This RACT/BACT/LAER Clearinghouse (Clearinghouse)[1] is capable of capturing and sharing information on NSR permits that have been issued. The Clearinghouse allows for web-based data entry (along with other methods of entry). The Clearinghouse is accessible to permitting authorities, the regulated community and the public via the internet as a tool to determine the best air pollution control technology for a given type of industrial facility. However, as your draft report accurately points out, the Clearinghouse database does not capture all NSR permits. This is because state and local agencies, which issue the large majority of NSR permits, are required by law to enter information about their permit determinations into the Clearinghouse only for nonattainment NSR permits. Data entry for PSD permits is voluntary. As a result, some agencies either do not enter all of their permits or they fail to enter permit data in a timely manner. We estimate that the Clearinghouse captures roughly 50 percent of all major source air permits. Nevertheless, the Clearinghouse is an accessible and user-friendly tool that centrally tracks a large cross-section of nationwide permit data. While there is no legal requirement to include PSD permits in the Clearinghouse, we have taken steps to improve participation. As an example, many of our EPA Regional Offices have Clean Air Act (CAA) section 105 Air Planning Agreements with their states that stipulate that the state must input data from all permits into the Clearinghouse, with some Regional Offices specifying a certain timeframe after permit issuance for completion of this task. We will continue to encourage better participation of the Clearinghouse by the state and local agencies.

Also, we appreciate that GAO's draft report recognizes that each of our Regional Offices track the step-by-step progress of permits within their areas of jurisdiction. The tracking of these permits is an important tool that enables Regional Offices to conduct proper oversight of permitting agencies in their states. The EPA, in this case, believes it is appropriate for those closest to the information to be responsible for that information. It is not necessary for a more detailed level of permit tracking to become centralized, because the Regional Offices, not EPA Headquarters, provide the oversight of the state and local programs. The EPA believes that to separately have an EPA-wide compilation of all of the Regional Offices' data would be redundant and, relative to the cost of its creation and maintenance, would add little benefit to this oversight function.

We also believe that a centralized data base of air permits would not help most members of the public, who typically are interested in a particular pending or issued permit near where they live rather than the universe of all permits in the country. Most states agencies and EPA Regional Offices maintain permitting websites that make it possible for members of the public to obtain information on specific issued permits or permits under review once they know which agency is responsible for permitting. [The EPA maintains a webpage called "Where You Live" (http://www.epa.gov/nsr/where.html), which enables anyone to identify the permitting authority for their area of interest, and to find contact names, phone numbers and links to that agency's website providing information on permits.

Finally, we note that a consistent theme in the draft GAO report is that the EPA's lack of centralized, comprehensive permitting data leads to difficulties in ensuring compliance or identifying instances of noncompliance. From our experience, such a relationship does not exist between permit tracking and identifying noncompliance, since most NSR noncompliance is related to sources that failed to apply for a permit when they should have. Stakeholders are alert to bring possible instances of an improperly issued permit to the EPA's or a court's attention, and only infrequently is an issued permit determined by the EPA or by a court not to comply with the CAA and EPA permitting rules. Thus, having more

---

[1] Best Available Control Technology (BACT) and Lowest Achievable Emissions Rate (LAER) are the control levels required in the attainment and nonattainment parts of the major NSR program, respectively. Reasonably Available Control Technology (RACT) is the minimum requirement that EPA can accept for existing major sources in nonattainment areas.

knowledge about facilities that received a preconstruction permit does not translate to knowing which facilities *should have applied for* a permit for their construction. As the draft report acknowledges, getting data on noncompliant sources is a highly resource- and time-consuming process, but having more centralized data on permit applications or final permits would not address the challenges that permitting authorities and enforcement staff face in ensuring that sources obtain permits when required. The facts that would indicate noncompliance are not usually publicly available and therefore must be obtained by way of specific letters to the source under our CAA section 114 authority. Consequently, a comprehensive and publicly available permits tracking database would likely provide little support to an investigation of a source for noncompliance.

Recommendation: *Using appropriate methods, such as sampling or periodic assessments, develop a process for evaluating the effects of [the EPA's] comments on draft NSR permits.*

Response: As GAO explains in the draft report, one part of the EPA's oversight of the NSR program is the EPA Regional Office-provided comments on draft NSR permits issued by states and local permitting agencies. In commenting on these draft permits, the EPA is not seeking to substitute its judgment for the state or local agency's, but rather to ensure that the individual permitting decisions are reasoned and faithful to the requirements of the CAA and the applicable NSR regulations and interpretations.

The EPA already implements the type of process described in this recommendation. As the draft report acknowledges, the EPA Regional Offices evaluate how their comments were considered by a state or local permitting authority in arriving at the final permit. Furthermore, during the draft permit development stage, it is common for there to be a robust interaction between EPA Regions and the relevant state to ensure that the permit complies with EPA rules and policy. Such advance interaction tends to reduce some of the need for EPA comments when the draft permit is made available for public comment. Additionally, the EPA Regions often conduct periodic assessments of the state and local permitting programs that they oversee. In these assessments, the Regional Offices evaluate whether the state is meeting the commitments of the applicable delegation agreement or complying with the approved state implementation plan, as applicable, and raise issues and concerns with the state, including whether the Regional Office believes that the permitting authority is not adequately considering EPA comments on its draft permits.

In closing, the EPA is committed to ensuring that the NSR permitting program is working as efficiently and effectively as possible. Thank you again for the opportunity to review and respond to the draft GAO report. If you have any questions, please contact David Svendsgaard at (919) 541-2380.

Sincerely,

[signature]

f.

Gina McCarthy
Assistant Administrator

Enclosure

Enclosure
EPA Detailed Comments on Draft GAO Report
"Air Pollution: EPA Needs Better Information on New Source Review Permits"
GAO Report: GAO-12-590

EPA recommends GAO make the following corrective and clarifying edits (in **RED** text) for the reasons given (in **BOLD** text).

"Highlights" Page

- "State and local permitting agencies track the NSR permits they issue, and EPA Regions track the permits the Regions issue, but EPA does not maintain complete ~~or~~and centralized information on all permits, despite a 2006 recommendation by the National Research Council that it do so." **This statement should acknowledge that EPA Regions track the permits the Regions issue. The other edits are added for consistency with other references in the draft report.**

- "EPA maintains several databases that compile data on draft and issued NSR permits, but these sources are incomplete and therefore cannot be used to identify all of the NSR permits that have been issued nationwide." **These edits are added for clarification.**

- "In addition, EPA has the opportunity to review and comment on every draft NSR permit issued by state and local permitting agencies, but it does not ~~track~~ systematically compile data on whether the permitting agencies address EPA's comments in final permits." **EPA is concerned that the use of the term "track" in this sentence could be misleading, since EPA does determine how state and local agencies address our comments on individual permits.**

- "~~The absence of more complete information on NSR permitting makes it difficult for EPA to know which units have obtained NSR permits or to assess how state and local permitting agencies vary from EPA in their interpretations of NSR requirements.~~" **EPA recommends deleting or rewording this sentence. Although EPA has not compiled in a centralized location comprehensive NSR permit information, EPA generally knows "which units have obtained NSR permits", since this information can be found on EPA Regional Office and state websites. We do not believe that having such data compiled in one location (i.e., EPA Headquarters) would provide any advantage over having each Region assess it at its level.**

- "Available data, although incomplete, suggest that a substantial number of generating units did not comply with requirements to obtain NSR permits." **Given the two previous paragraphs on this page, it is unclear whether "available data, although incomplete" refers to permits data or to other types of data that EPA would use to identify noncompliance. Throughout the report, it would be helpful if GAO could more clearly distinguish between NSR permits information, which the draft report suggests should be better tracked by EPA, and facility information that would assist in enforcement investigations. The two types of information are fundamentally different.**

1

Page 2

- "Units built before August 7, 1977, ~~are not~~ have not been required to undergo…" **Tense correction.**

Page 6

- "Although this report focuses on NSR, the Clean Air Act and its implementing regulations subject electric generating units to additional emissions control requirements." **Throughout the draft report, GAO uses "electric generating units" in some cases, and "generating units" in other cases. For clarity and consistency, we recommend the report only use the term "electric generating units".**

Pages 6-7

- "State and local permitting agencies track the NSR permits they issue, and EPA Regions track the permits the Regions issue (and often the permits of their state and local agencies as well), but EPA does not maintain data on these permits in a complete and centralized database, which limits its ability to assess the impact of NSR." **It is unclear how compiling permits from different permitting agencies into a centralized database would enable EPA to "assess the impact of NSR." Unlike other EPA programs, NSR is not an emissions reduction program; it is a program that minimizes the emissions increases resulting from the construction and operation of new and modified facilities. In order to understand the impact of NSR, you have to determine the baseline emissions for a given facility, which would mean determining what state or local requirements apply, in addition to the federal requirements. For any given permit, it would be a very case-specific analysis. Therefore, it would still be difficult to determine the impact of the NSR program from centrally compiled permit data.**

- "In addition, EPA has the opportunity to review and comment on every draft NSR permit issued by state and local permitting agencies, but the agency does not track the extent to which permitting authorities address EPA's comments. The absence of this information makes it difficult for EPA to measure the impact of its comments and may impede EPA ability to assess how state and local permitting agencies may differ from EPA in their interpretation of NSR requirements." **It is important to note that many states implement their own regulations under their state implementation plan. In these cases, it is not unrealistic that the state's regulatory or policy interpretation may differ from EPA's.**

Page 9

- "However, the database is incomplete; EPA officials said it contains information on approximately 50 percent of issued permits …" **This edit is added for clarification, since the "50 percent" value is an EPA estimate.**

2

- "Because EPA does not maintain comprehensive information on the NSR permits issued to fossil fuel electric generating units across the nation, the agency does not have complete data on which units have obtained permits, which limits its ability to assess the scope and impact of NSR. Without such data, EPA is unable to fully assess what controls have been required or estimate what emissions from generating units may have been averted as a result of NSR requirements." **As noted above, determining the impact of NSR, or the emissions that have been averted as a result of NSR, is a very case-specific analysis. To the extent that EPA has adequate information to perform this challenging task, it would be better performed by each of the ten EPA Regions, who have closer access and more familiarity with the state and local agency permits.**

Page 10

- "In addition, the absence of information on NSR permits hinders EPA's ability to efficiently target noncompliance." **EPA does not agree with the conclusion that links the lack of comprehensive permits data to the challenges EPA faces in identifying noncompliance. Most NSR noncompliance is from not getting a permit when the source should have applied for a permit. Thus, having more information on permitted facilities would not necessarily help identify noncompliant sources.**

Page 11

- "Officials we interviewed in several EPA regional offices said they note the response of state and local permitting agencies to EPA's comments, but all said that they do not regularly report this information to EPA headquarters... However, without compiling any information on whether state and local permitting agencies have incorporated its comments into final NSR permits, EPA is limited in its ability to assess the impact of these comments on state and local permitting decisions across the nation. For example, EPA cannot assess the extent to which NSR emissions control requirements imposed by state and local permitting agencies may differ from those suggested by EPA in its comments." **Same as previous comment on pp. 6-7. While EPA recognizes the importance of determining how a state responded to our comments on a draft permit, EPA strongly believes that this function is inherently the responsibility of each Region.**

- Footnote 20: "... no less stringent ~~that~~than EPA's regulations." **Typographical correction.**

Page 14

- **Footnote 22 refers to an EPA rule proposed in 2006 but never finalized. This statement does not accurately characterize the 2006 "debottlenecking" rule proposal, since it was never intended "to clarify how emissions decreases from a project may be included in the netting calculation..." However, EPA did issue clarifying guidance on this topic in April 2011 (http://www.epa.gov/region07/air/nsr/nsrmemos/atpanet.pdf), so we suggest that GAO instead refers to it.**

3

Page 21

- In this "Conclusions" section, GAO appears to again tie together the idea that having better permit data will improve compliance with NSR requirements. However, most noncompliance with NSR results from facilities not getting required permits, which means that having more information on permitted facilities would not necessarily help identify noncompliant sources.

4

Appendix V: GAO Contacts and Staff Acknowledgments

GAO Contacts	David C. Trimble, (202) 512-3841 or trimbled@gao.gov Frank Rusco, (202) 512-3841 or ruscof@gao.gov
Staff Acknowledgments	In addition to the individuals named above, Michael Hix (Assistant Director), Ellen W. Chu, Philip Farah, Cindy Gilbert, Jessica Lemke, Jon Ludwigson, Nancy Meyer, Mick Ray, and Jeanette Soares made key contributions to this report.

GAO's Mission	The Government Accountability Office, the audit, evaluation, and investigative arm of Congress, exists to support Congress in meeting its constitutional responsibilities and to help improve the performance and accountability of the federal government for the American people. GAO examines the use of public funds; evaluates federal programs and policies; and provides analyses, recommendations, and other assistance to help Congress make informed oversight, policy, and funding decisions. GAO's commitment to good government is reflected in its core values of accountability, integrity, and reliability.
Obtaining Copies of GAO Reports and Testimony	The fastest and easiest way to obtain copies of GAO documents at no cost is through GAO's website (www.gao.gov). Each weekday afternoon, GAO posts on its website newly released reports, testimony, and correspondence. To have GAO e-mail you a list of newly posted products, go to www.gao.gov and select "E-mail Updates."
Order by Phone	The price of each GAO publication reflects GAO's actual cost of production and distribution and depends on the number of pages in the publication and whether the publication is printed in color or black and white. Pricing and ordering information is posted on GAO's website, http://www.gao.gov/ordering.htm. Place orders by calling (202) 512-6000, toll free (866) 801-7077, or TDD (202) 512-2537. Orders may be paid for using American Express, Discover Card, MasterCard, Visa, check, or money order. Call for additional information.
Connect with GAO	Connect with GAO on Facebook, Flickr, Twitter, and YouTube. Subscribe to our RSS Feeds or E-mail Updates. Listen to our Podcasts. Visit GAO on the web at www.gao.gov.
To Report Fraud, Waste, and Abuse in Federal Programs	Contact: Website: www.gao.gov/fraudnet/fraudnet.htm E-mail: fraudnet@gao.gov Automated answering system: (800) 424-5454 or (202) 512-7470
Congressional Relations	Katherine Siggerud, Managing Director, siggerudk@gao.gov, (202) 512-4400, U.S. Government Accountability Office, 441 G Street NW, Room 7125, Washington, DC 20548
Public Affairs	Chuck Young, Managing Director, youngc1@gao.gov, (202) 512-4800 U.S. Government Accountability Office, 441 G Street NW, Room 7149 Washington, DC 20548